STORMS

Written and edited by **Jenny Wood**

TWO-CAN

STORMS

First published 1990 by
Two-Can Publishing
27 Cowper Street
London EC2A 4AP

© Two-Can Publishing 1990
© Text Jenny Wood 1990
Design by Claire Legemah

Printed in Portugal

British Library Cataloguing in Publication Data
Wood, Jenny
Storms.
1. Storms
I. Title
551.5'5

ISBN 1-85434-022-0

Photograph Credits:
p.5 Tony Stone Associates Ltd; p.6 Robert Harding Picture Library; p.7 (top) Zefa, (bottom) The Meteorological Office/ETH Zurich; p.9 (inset) Science Photo Library, Bruce
Coleman; p.10 Zefa; p.10/11 Explorer; p.11 Tony Stone Associates Ltd; p.12 (inset) GeoScience Features Picture Library; p.12/13 Zefa; p.14 Topham Picture Source; p.15 (top)
Rex Features, (bottom) Science Photo Library; p.16/17 Survival Anglia Photo Library; p.17 (inset) The Hutchinson Library; p.18 The Meteorological Office/Colin Crane; p.22
Science Photo Library; p.23 (top) Topham Picture Source, (bottom) The Telegraph Colour Library; Cover photo (front) Zefa; Cover photo (back) Robert Harding Picture
Library.

Illustration Credits:
p.4, 5, 7, 8, 11, 13, 14, 18, 19, 20, 21, 22, Francis Mosley; p.24-28, Linden Artists/Francis Phillipps.

CONTENTS

WHAT IS A STORM?

Flashes of lightning, loud crashes of thunder, torrential rain, howling winds, driving snow! Those may be some of the things the word 'storm' conjures up in your mind. A storm is a period of very bad, often violent weather. It may include rain, hail, snow, thunder and lightning, strong winds or a mixture of these.

Weather is caused by changes in the thin blanket of air, called the **atmosphere**, which surrounds the Earth. Movements of hot and cold air as well as changes in the amount of moisture in the air mean that the atmosphere varies between being hot or cold, dry or wet, calm or windy.

Sometimes huge masses of air settle over areas of sea or land. These **air masses** become warm, cold, dry or damp, depending on the nature of the land or sea below. They bring days, even weeks of unchanging weather.

When these air masses begin to move, the problems begin! Different air masses don't mix, and if the edge or **front** of a warm air mass meets a cold air mass, or vice versa, storms are likely to occur.

▶ Dark storm clouds gathering at sunset.

clouds form

rain, hail and snow

air cools

Sun's rays heat up the Earth

▼ As the Sun's rays warm the Earth, heat and moisture are released into the atmosphere. This moisture produces clouds, rain, hail and snow.

cold air is pulled in from behind

warm, moist air rises

When cold and warm air masses meet, clouds form along each front and there are violent storms.

RAIN AND HAILSTORMS

Raindrops form when tiny water droplets in a cloud join together or when ice crystals in a cloud melt. When the raindrops become too large and heavy for the air to support them, they start to fall out of the cloud. The larger the raindrops, the faster they fall!

Hailstones are formed in much the same way as raindrops but they fall only from **cumulonimbus** clouds. The inside of a cumulonimbus cloud is very cold and the hailstones start their lives as ice particles. As these particles are thrown about inside the cloud they absorb water droplets which then freeze to them in layers, like an onion. As many as 25 layers have been found on a single hailstone!

DID YOU KNOW?

● Most hailstones which fall are about the size of a pea, but the largest hailstone ever recorded was the size of a melon and weighed 758g (27 ounces). It fell in Coffeyville, Kansas, USA on September 3rd 1970.

● The driest place in the world is the desert town of Arica in Chile. It receives only about 0.76 mm (0.03 inches) of rain each year!

● The wettest place in the world is Mount Wai-'ale-'ale in Hawaii. It has rain for about 335 days of the year!

◀ Rainstorms are short periods of very heavy rain which fall over a small area. They are often accompanied by thunder and can cause **flash floods** as rivers become torrents.

▶ This cross-section of a hailstone shows the many different layers of ice.

▲ Light rays travel in straight lines but when sunlight shines through raindrops, the rays bend slightly. White light is actually made up of seven different coloured lights and each one bends in a different way. So the light splits into red, orange, yellow, green, blue, indigo and violet. This causes a rainbow to appear.

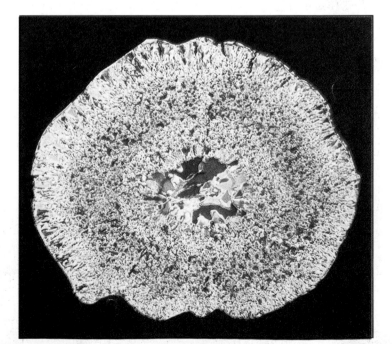

THUNDER AND LIGHTNING

Most thunderstorms happen in summer, when the air is warm and damp. As the air rises, it cools, and the moisture it contains forms huge, grey-black thunderclouds.

Fast-moving air currents inside each thundercloud cause electric charges to build up. Eventually, the electricity is released from the clouds in the form of giant sparks which we know as lightning.

When a flash of lightning leaves a cloud, it zig-zags to the ground. It then returns, racing up the same path back to the cloud. It is the bright light of this **return stroke** that we see.

Return strokes travel at about the speed of light. They discharge almost 100 million volts of electricity and heat the air in their paths to over 33,000°C (60,000°F). The heated air expands quickly and collides with cool air, producing sound waves that we hear as thunder.

Lightning is produced when separated positive and negative electrical charges flow towards one another. As well as zig-zagging to the ground, lightning can occur within a cloud or between clouds.

DID YOU KNOW?

● You can tell how far away a thunderstorm is. Every 5 seconds between a lightning flash and a thunderclap counts as 2 km (1.2 miles) in distance.

● Long ago people believed that thunder and lightning were signs that their gods were angry. Thor, the Norse god of thunder, was thought to race across the sky in a chariot brewing up storms by blowing through his beard.

● Throughout the world there are about 16 million thunderstorms each year, and 100 flashes of lightning every second.

▶ Thunderclouds often stretch several thousand metres up into the atmosphere. The fast-moving air currents inside them can hold extra-large raindrops, so thunderclouds often produce heavy rain.

▲ Thunder and lightning happen at the same time, but because light travels faster than sound, we see lightning before we hear thunder.

SNOWSTORMS

When water droplets freeze on to ice particles in a cloud, the particles get bigger and become ice crystals. As these fall through the cloud, they collide with other ice crystals and become snowflakes.

Once the snowflakes are large and heavy enough, they begin to fall out of the cloud. If they fall through warmer air they melt and fall as rain. But if the air is cold they fall as snow. Snow can soon start to cause problems on the ground. A snowfall of only 10cm (4 inches) is enough to block roads!

A severe snowstorm is called a blizzard. These occur when snowfall is accompanied by strong winds which whip up the snow into a swirling white mist and blow it into deep piles called snowdrifts. Poor visibility and near-freezing temperatures make life very difficult in blizzard conditions.

Machines called snowploughs and snowblowers are used to clear roads

▲ Most snow crystals have six sides. Although billions of them have fallen on to the Earth, no two look exactly the same. Different weather conditions produce different shaped crystals. Needle and rod shapes form in cold air. The more complicated shapes form in warmer air.

▲ When heavy snow falls, animals often have difficulty in finding food. Farmers sometimes have to take bales of hay out to the fields.

DID YOU KNOW?

● The most snow to fall in a year was at Paradise, Mount Rainier, USA in the winter of 1971. About 31m (1,224 inches) fell, enough to reach a third of the way up the Statue of Liberty!

● 'Super Frosty', the world's biggest snowman, was built by a team of people in Alaska between 20 February and 5 March 1988. He stood 19.37m (63.56 feet) high!

after severe snowstorms, but even they can find it difficult to clear deep snow from remote areas. People who live in these places can be 'snowed in' for days, even weeks. Even in large cities, daily life can be disrupted by heavy snowfall.

But snow does have its uses. It is an important source of water. When it melts in the mountains, it provides water for streams, **hydroelectric** power plants and **reservoirs**. It also helps protect plants and hibernating animals from the cold winter air.

STORMS AT SEA

The sea never stops moving because the air above it is never still. The wind makes ripples and waves on the sea's surface. As the wind gets stronger, the waves become bigger and very strong winds can whip the surface of the sea into a terrifying mass of spray. Storm waves are powerful and out at sea they may rise higher than 12m (40 feet). They can pick up huge boulders and throw them far up on the shore. They can even hurl large ships against rocks and smash them.

▼ Storms can cause problems for ships at sea.

The largest waves are called **tsunamis** (a Japanese word meaning 'overflowing waves'). These are not caused by wind but by underwater volcanic explosions or earthquakes which cause the sea floor to rise and fall. Tsunamis travel quickly, at up to 800km (500 miles) per hour. Where the sea bed gets shallower, they slow down but become higher. A tsunami can form a wall of water more than 24m (80 feet) high when it approaches shallow water near shore. If a tsunami reaches land, it can swamp large areas and cause terrible damage.

Wind causes waves which form far out to sea. The wind pushes the water particles which move round and round. Near the coast, where the water is shallow, the sea bed interferes with the movement of the water. Then the top of the wave breaks on to the beach.

HURRICANES, TYPHOONS AND CYCLONES

Violent, whirling storms which begin over warm oceans are known by different names in different parts of the world. In the Caribbean they are called **hurricanes**, in the China Seas **typhoons** and in the Indian Ocean **cyclones**. Storm clouds, rain and howling winds of up to 300 km (190 miles) per hour race across the sky, stirring up huge waves on the surface of the sea below.

When one of these tropical storms moves over land, strong winds and heavy rain hit the area for several hours. Fields, even towns may be flooded, trees and crops uprooted and buildings destroyed. Sometimes, many people are killed. Gradually the storm dies down until at last it blows itself out.

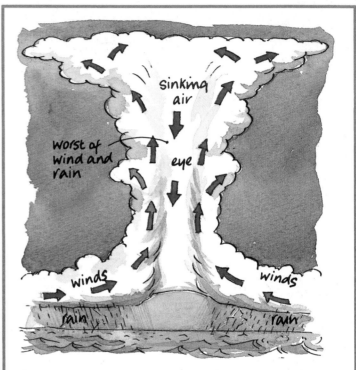

Most tropical storms develop in summer, when the seas and the air above are at their warmest. As the sea heats the air, a current of warm, moist air rises above the water. Winds rush in below this air current and whirl upwards. As they rise, they cool, and the huge amounts of water vapour they contain form towering clouds. At the centre of the storm is a calm area known as the **eye**. In a circle immediately around the eye, the wind and rain are at their fiercest. Although the air in the eye is hotter than in the rest of the storm, it does not rise. Instead, it sinks slowly down to the surface of the sea.

◀ The fierce winds of a tropical storm have blown this plane right out of the sky. It has landed in an area flooded by the storm's heavy rain.

▲ Palm trees battered by the winds of an approaching tropical storm.

▼ This photograph, taken from the American space shuttle *Discovery*, shows the whirling clouds of a hurricane. Right in the centre of the storm you can see the calm 'eye'.

SAND AND DUSTSTORMS

Wind blowing over a sandy area such as a desert or a dry river bed picks up sand and carries it through the air, creating a sandstorm. Most of the sand stays about 51cm (20 inches) above the ground, although some grains can rise to a height of about 2 m (6 feet). During a sandstorm, the sand seems to jump along as the grains bang against each other and then bounce up into the air.

Sandstorms can be a danger to desert travellers. The stinging clouds of sand can clog machinery and reduce visibility. They can also damage crops.

Some desert animals have special ways of protecting themselves against sandstorms. The camel, for instance, can close its nostrils and has a second set of eyelids to cover its eyes.

◀ Dust storms occur where the ground is very dry or has been badly farmed, resulting in bare soil with no vegetation to protect it. Thousands of tonnes of dusty soil are carried high into the air by strong winds and blown away. Dust storms help to cause **soil erosion** and can strip all the fertile earth away from a large area.

TORNADOES

A **tornado** is a violent, twisting, whirlwind which forms over land and is often accompanied by heavy rain, thunder and lightning. It looks like a funnel-shaped cloud reaching downwards from the base of a cumulonimbus cloud. Tornadoes form in warm, moist air where winds blow into each other from opposite directions. A whirling column of hot air is created which spins at tremendous speed until it stretches from the cloud to the ground.

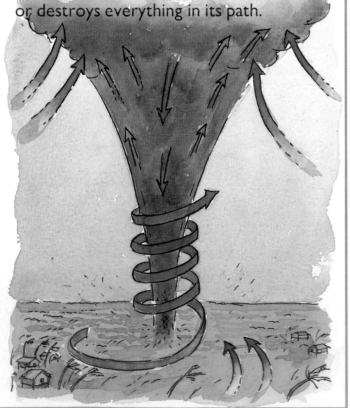

As the whirling column of the tornado hurtles over the ground at speeds of up to 97 km (60 miles) per hour, the strong upward current of air at its centre sucks up or destroys everything in its path.

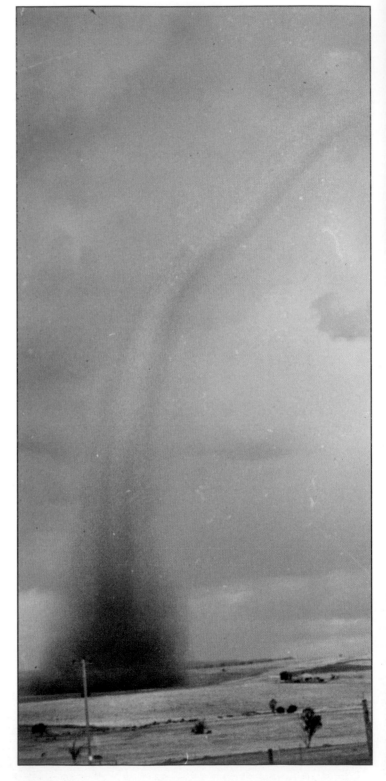

▲ Tornadoes are the most destructive winds that occur on our planet. They are most common in the USA.

MAKE A WEATHER STATION

By measuring and recording changes in the weather, you can forecast the weather like scientists do.

RAIN GAUGE

It's easy to measure how much rain falls, with the help of a rain gauge.

You need:
- A flat-bottomed glass jar or bottle
- A plastic funnel with the same diameter as the jar or bottle
- A ruler

Place the funnel in the jar. Use the ruler to measure the amount of rainfall.

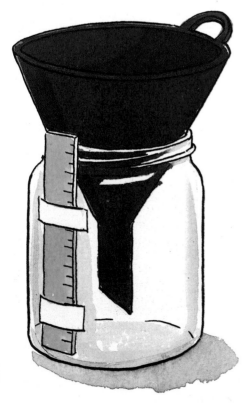

BAROMETER

A **barometer** measures the amount of air pressing down on the Earth. A rise in pressure is a sign of good weather, but if the pressure drops, look out for storms!

You need:
- A jam jar with a wide neck
- A balloon
- Scissors
- A thick rubber band
- A drinking straw
- A needle
- Sticky tape and glue
- A piece of card
- A ruler and a pen
- Plasticine

1 Cut off the neck of the balloon. Stretch the rest of the balloon tightly over the neck of the jar. Use the rubber band to hold it in place.

2 Tape the needle to one end of the straw. Glue the other end to the centre of the balloon.

3 Mark off a scale on the card. Push the card into the plasticine, then place it just behind the point of the needle. The needle will move up and down the scale as the air pressure changes.

WIND SOCK

A wind sock tells you from which direction the wind is blowing. It will also give you a rough idea of the wind's speed.

You need:
- A piece of lightweight cloth, 1m x 1m (3 feet x 3 feet)
- Scissors
- A needle and thread
- A wire coathanger
- A curtain ring
- Strong card
- A felt pen (with waterproof ink)
- An old broom handle
- Drawing pins
- A garden cane, 60-70 cm (24-30 inches)
- Strong string
- A compass

1 Cut out a 'sock' shape from your material and sew the straight edges together.

2 Bend the coathanger into a circle. Squeeze the hook until it forms a small ring. Slip the curtain ring on to the wire circle at the side opposite the hook.

3 Fold the wide curved edge of the sock over the wire circle and stitch it into place. Leave the hook and the curtain ring sticking out.

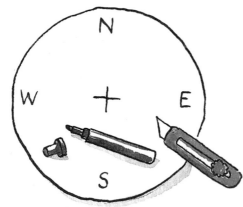

4 Cut out a circle about 30 cm (12 inches) in diameter from the card. Make two slits in the centre of the circle large enough to allow the card to fit tightly on to the broom handle. Write the letters N, E, S, W on the underside of the circle, to act as points of the compass.

5 Slide the circle on to the broom handle and pin in position.

6 Slide the garden cane through the curtain ring and wire hook. Tie the cane firmly to the broom handle.

THERMOMETER

A **thermometer** measures the temperature of the air.

You need:
- A glass bottle with a screw top
- Water
- Coloured ink
- A drinking straw
- Plasticine
- A piece of card
- A ruler
- A pen
- Sticky tape

1 Fill the bottle right to the top with water coloured by a little ink.

2 Ask an adult to make a hole (just large enough for the straw) in the screw top.

3 Fix the screw top tightly in position and push the straw through the hole. Put plasticine round the straw.

4 Make a card scale and tape it to the back of the straw.

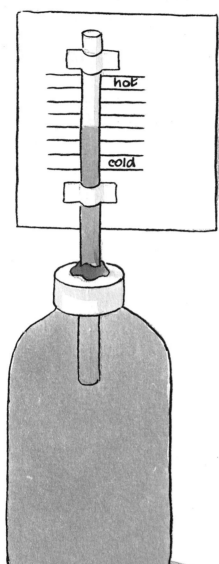

As the temperature rises and falls, the coloured water will move up and down the straw, giving you a rough guide as to how much hotter or colder the air temperature has become.

Setting up

Dig a hole in the ground for your rain gauge, away from trees and bushes if possible. Your barometer will work indoors or outdoors, but don't place it in the sun. Tie the wind sock to a fence post, or to the roof of a shed or garage. It should be at least 2m (7 feet) above ground. Keep it away from any trees and buildings that might prevent the wind blowing freely. Your thermometer needs to be in a shady place outdoors.

Check all the measurements two or three times a day. Keep a log book with your results.

time	air pressure		wind direction	temperature	rainfall	remarks
	pressure	trend				
			S.W.	rising	none	cloudy morning
8am	high	falling / steady	S.W.	rising	5mm	rain at midday, sun trying to break through
1pm	average	rising	W.	falling	none	clear, dry evening
	average					

SCIENCE AT WORK

Every hour of the day and night, weather stations all round the world are recording facts and figures about the weather. Temperatures, wind direction, wind speed, cloud cover, rainfall and **air pressure** are all measured, and the information transmitted to a national weather office. There, weather scientists, or **meteorologists**, draw up a map called a **synoptic chart**. Each local weather station is marked on this map by a circle. The information it has sent in is marked around it, using coded symbols which are recognised all over the world.

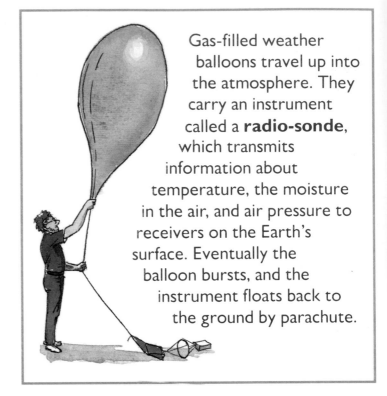

Gas-filled weather balloons travel up into the atmosphere. They carry an instrument called a **radio-sonde**, which transmits information about temperature, the moisture in the air, and air pressure to receivers on the Earth's surface. Eventually the balloon bursts, and the instrument floats back to the ground by parachute.

CANE GILBERT
15 1988
EDT
TEXAS
MISSISSIPPI
ALABAMA
GEORGIA

◀ Satellites are especially helpful in detecting hurricanes over tropical oceans. Meteorologists are now more easily able to chart a storm's progress.

▼ Some weather satellites orbit the Earth, moving from Pole to Pole. Others become stationary over a fixed place on the Equator. The television cameras they carry scan the Earth below, then transmit signals to receivers on the Earth's surface. These signals can be changed into pictures.

When the synoptic chart is complete, the information is fed into a computer. The computer then prints out maps which forecast how weather conditions are likely to change in the following days.

Measuring instruments such as weather balloons and satellites have allowed meteorologists to discover many new things about the weather. The use of computers means that they can find out what the weather is like in any part of the world at any given time. The result is more accurate weather forecasting.

◀ Weather satellites take photographs of the Earth from space. These photographs show the cloud cover over different parts of the Earth's surface, and help meteorologists to trace the development and movement of cloud systems.

THE HURRICANE

Father turned off the radio. 'Hurricane warning,' he told them. 'Come on. You know what to do.'

It took them nearly an hour to fasten all the shutters securely and move the garden furniture into the house. By the time they had finished it had started to get dark. A huge mass of iron-grey clouds filled the sky to the east, towering above the mud-coloured sea. The horizon was black, lit only by the distant flicker of lightning. The wind had started to rise, sweeping the dust off the streets. In the distance unfastened doors and shutters banged. Hurricane Dora was about to arrive.

'Everyone downstairs,' ordered Father. The family clattered down into the cellar and sat nervously in the darkened room. They knew there was not long to wait.

By ten o'clock the sky was black. Still no rain had fallen, but the wind had started to tear at the palm trees, bending them almost in two. In the bay below, the little fishing port disappeared in a thick fog of sea spray. Waves began to smash up the beach, spilling water on to the road beyond.

Ten minutes later the full force of the hurricane hit the island. The tidal wave which had been building up across the ocean surged into the bay. As the wave raced towards the land, it was pushed into the narrow space between the cliffs on either side of the bay, and it began to rise. By the time it reached the beach, the wall of water was over five metres high. It was unstoppable. It surged over the sand and crashed into the little painted wooden houses, sweeping them away like litter.

A fishing boat was somehow, miraculously, lifted out of the bay, carried over the town and dropped gently on to the roof of the fire station. There it remained, trapped by a mass of splintered timbers. An advertising board as big as a house whirled through the air like a playing card.

The noise of the wind was like the roar of a dozen aeroplane engines all revving up together. The wind had risen to about two hundred and forty kilometres an hour. It was strong enough to pick up humans like pieces of straw and whirl them away. At that speed it could even knock down the side of a house.

Hurricane Dora tore across the island, uprooting large trees and tossing them around like paper darts. She ripped the soil from the fields and churned it into brown mist. And then came the rain. The drops were enormous. It sounded as if someone was emptying a never-ending stream of gravel over the house.

Within minutes the ground had become a quagmire. Every hollow in the ground was filled with water. Water spilled out of the hollows and began to run downhill. Tracks became streams. Streams became torrents. The water raced downwards trying to reach the sea. It carved at the land, tearing out mud, boulders and trees. The river rose and within minutes had burst its banks. Dark brown water spilled out over the countryside.

The family, safe in their cellar, huddled together and listened to Dora's progress. Apart from an uncanny half hour of silence, when the eye of the hurricane passed over them, the wind and rain battered at the house for twelve hours.

Then, at last, Hurricane Dora had gone. The family climbed stiffly up the stairs and went outside. They gasped at the devastation they saw. Their garden had disappeared. In its place was a crazy chaos of smashed trees, upturned cars and bits of other people's houses. They turned and looked at their own house. The pink paint was covered with marks caused by flying objects. Charlotte pointed at the roof. Only three tiles remained in place.

Laura ran to the bottom of the garden and looked down on to the little fishing port below. 'Oh, no!' she gasped in horror. The rest of them peered down. The stone jetty was all that remained of the town. The houses had vanished. A few people had returned from their refuges in the hills and were walking about, searching for the remains of their homes.

'It will all be rebuilt,' Father assured them. 'This isn't the first hurricane to hit the island, and it won't be the last.'

'Yes,' added Mother. 'And thanks to the hurricane warning on the radio, it's unlikely that anyone was hurt. Everyone will have got to the hills in plenty of time.'

'Come on,' said Father. 'We've got a lot of tidying up to do. Let's get to work.'

From down below in the village came the sound of hammering, as people began to build new wooden houses.

TRUE OR FALSE?

Which of these facts are true and which ones are false?
If you have read this book carefully, you will know the answers.

1 A rainbow is a full circle of colour.

2 We always hear thunder before we see lightning.

3 The atmosphere is a thin blanket of air which surrounds the Earth.

4 Hailstones fall from any type of cloud.

5 Tsunami is another word for tornado.

6 Scientists who study weather are called meteorologists.

7 A snowfall of as little as 10 cm (4 inches) is enough to block roads.

8 An avalanche is caused by the movement of waves.

9 At the centre of a hurricane is a calm area known as the 'eye'.

10 The driest place in the world is Mount Wai-'ale-'ale in Hawaii.

11 Tornadoes emerge only from cumulonimbus clouds.

12 The strong winds of a dust storm can strip the ground of soil.

13 A thermometer measures air pressure.

GLOSSARY

Air mass is a huge area of air with the same temperature throughout.

Air pressure is the phrase used to describe the force of the air pushing down on the Earth. The amount of air pressure varies from place to place and it can change from day to day. Rising air pressure usually means that good weather is on the way; falling air pressure usually means that the weather will turn unpleasant.

Atmosphere is the thin blanket of air which surrounds the Earth.

Avalanche is a sudden fall of snow and ice down a steep slope. Avalanches are caused by disturbances such as heavy winds, earth tremors and explosions. They can be very dangerous to people and animals.

Barometer is the instrument used to measure air pressure.

Cumulonimbus is the name of a huge thundercloud which brings heavy rain, snow or hail. Cumulonimbus clouds often stretch high into the atmosphere, and their tops are made of ice crystals.

Cyclone is the word used in the area of the Indian Ocean to describe a tropical storm.

Eye is the name given to the calm area in the centre of a hurricane.

Flash flood is a severe flood which occurs after sudden, very heavy rain has caused rivers to burst their banks.

Front is the name given to the edge of an air mass.

Hurricane is the word used in the area of the Caribbean to describe a tropical storm.

Hydroelectricity is electricity which is produced by using water power.

Meteorologist is a scientist who studies the weather.

Radio-sonde is an instrument which is carried up into the atmosphere on a weather balloon. It transmits information about temperature, air pressure and the amount of moisture in the air back to receivers on the Earth's surface.

Reservoir is a large, man-made lake where water is stored before being treated and piped into people's homes.

Return stroke is the movement of a flash of lightning from the ground back up to the cloud from which it came. It is the bright light of the return stroke that we actually see.

Soil erosion is the stripping away of the top, fertile layer of soil. This can be caused by strong winds, for example, and heavy floods.

Synoptic chart is a type of weather map. It shows readings from every one of a country's weather stations and uses coded numbers, signs and symbols which are understood by meteorologists all over the world.

Thermometer is the instrument used to measure air temperature.

Tornado is a violent, twisting whirlwind which forms over land. It looks like a funnel-shaped cloud extending down from the base of a cumulonimbus cloud. It spins at tremendous speed over the ground and causes terrible damage.

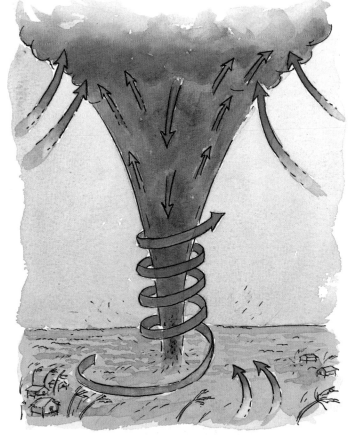

Tsunami is the name given to a huge wave caused by underwater volcanic explosions or earthquakes. If a tsunami reaches land, it can cause terrible damage.

Typhoon is the word used in the area of the China Seas to describe a tropical storm.

INDEX